14

8/231.

D0643727

INVENTORS & INVENTIONS

ROCKETS

INVENTORS & INVENTIONS

ROCKETS

MARY VIRGINIA FOX

BENCHMARK BOOKS

MARSHALL CAVENDISH
NEW YORK

Benchmark Books
Marshall Cavendish Corporation
99 White Plains Road
Tarrytown, New York 10591-9001

©Marshall Cavendish Corporation, 1996

Series created by The Creative Publishing Company

Library of Congress Cataloging-in-Publication Data

Fox, Mary Virginia.
    Rockets / Mary Virginia Fox.
        p.   cm. -- (Inventors & inventions)
    Includes index.
    Summary: An introduction to the science of rocketry from the time
of the earliest Chinese rockets in A.D. 1231 to the present.
    ISBN 0-7614-0063-X
    1. Rocketry--History--Juvenile literature.   [1. Rocketry.]
I. Title.   II. Series.
TL782.5.F69   1995
621.43'56'09--dc20

                                            95-15271
                                              CIP
                                              AC

Printed and bound in Hong Kong

Acknowledgments

Technical Consultant: Teodoro C. Robles, Ph.D.
Illustrations on pages 25, 27 and 29 by Julian Baker

The publishers would like to thank the following for their permission to reproduce photographs:
Mary Evans Picture Library, (11, 14, 24, 31); The Hulton Deutsch Collection, (30, 41); Image Select, (frontispiece); NASA, (46, 56, 57); Science & Society Picture Library, (9, 18, 33, 34, 36, 39, 40, 43, 44); Science Photo Library Ltd., (NASA front cover, 7, 23, 32, 35, 45, 47, 50, 51, 55, Roger Ressmeyer/Starlight 26, 28, 58, 59); UPI/Bettmann, (12, 13, 16, 17, 21, 22, 48, 53).

(Cover) Space shuttle Atlantis *lifts off on a mission to place a satellite in space in April, 1991.*

(Frontispiece) A Saturn IB *rocket at Kennedy Space Center, Florida, ready to take the first crew to the* Skylab *space station in May, 1973.*

Contents

—— Chapter 1 ——
Now and Then

The space shuttle is an awesome sight, sitting on its "tail" ready for launch. That tail contains three of the most powerful rocket engines ever built. The shuttle's stubby wings are swept far back from the cockpit. Two long, pencil-shaped rockets on either side of the main craft, or orbiter, provide most of the power to lift its 4.4 million pounds into space. When these power packages are empty, the rockets descend by parachute and are later retrieved from the ocean by salvage ships.

Only the big belly tank, a raw amber in color, will burn up in the atmosphere. If it had been painted to match the rest of the craft, that paint would have added an unnecessary six hundred pounds of weight. Every ounce of load to be carried into space requires extra pounds of fuel to get it there. All the calculations have been precise.

Thirty-two thousand cinderlike insulation tiles cover the entire body of the orbiter. These protect it from the searing heat upon reentry into Earth's atmosphere.

The countdown for liftoff starts long before the astronauts enter the craft. Every throttle, every valve is checked and tested five times a second. Any abnormality shows up on the flashing control panels in the shuttle and at Mission Control in Houston.

The computers command the three rocket engines to fire with a mighty roar. The spacecraft shudders for a few seconds, still held down on the launch pad. Tons of water pour onto the launch pad, not only to reduce the searing heat, but to block excess vibrations from the giant rocket engines. There is a burst of flames and a billow of steam. Then the solid booster rockets ignite.

(Opposite) A space shuttle climbs away from the Earth, powered on the first stage of its journey by the two large solid-fuel booster rockets and the shuttle's own three main rockets.

The launch tower drops off and the shuttle rises. Though the action seems to be in slow motion, the rockets gain speed, and the astronauts are shooting through the sky, a trail of white vapor tracking them. When the boosters have burned all their propellant, they detach and fall into the ocean below.

The shuttle is now arcing upside down over the ocean. The last acceleration comes five minutes later and lasts a minute. The big belly tank is now empty of its 526,616 gallons of liquid hydrogen and oxygen, which were consumed in less than ten minutes. It drops off to further lighten the load. Now two other engines ignite at the rear of the orbiter, but they are midgets by comparison to the discarded rocket engines that sent the space shuttle on its journey at 17,400 miles per hour.

The power of these rocket engines and those still on the drawing board is making it possible for us to explore space. Someday we will surely settle new worlds, but this would not have been possible without the imagination of others who came before us.

The First Explosions

Sometime at least two thousand years ago, somewhere in China, someone lit a fire that caused an explosion and made history. It could have been an accident as a pile of yellow sand and a mound of white powder were scuffed into the ashes of a fire.

The yellow sand was sulfur. Abandoned wells in this dry part of the world contain this chemical, which evaporates into a sandy substance. The white powder was saltpeter, a form of nitrate of potassium, which forms naturally on rocks. Combined with the charcoal of the fire, it made a spectacular explosion.

It was not long before someone packed the lethal ingredients into a bamboo tube and lit a fuse. When the force of the explosion was directed through one narrow opening, the rocket shot through the air. The same thing happens when you blow up a balloon and suddenly let loose the one escape valve — the balloon will shoot off on its own.

We know that the earliest rockets were made in China because people wrote about them. When Mongol soldiers besieged the town of Kaifeng-fu in A.D. 1231, the townsfolk drove them away with "fiery arrows." These arrows were said to have "made a noise like thunder and traveled great distances." Arab traders brought gunpowder to the Middle East, and from there word spread quickly to Europe. World traveler Marco Polo brought back his own stories of Chinese rockets.

Rockets Become Dangerous Weapons

It was not until the seventeenth century that English scientist, Sir Isaac Newton , in his Third Law, explained what was happening — that for every action there is an equal and opposite reaction. The explosive power from the tail of a rocket equals the thrust, or forward force, that sends the rocket upward.

Knowing this in the 1800s, William Congreve of England made plans for his own form of weaponry. Congreve had

---

AMAZING FACTS

The world's first would-be astronaut was a Chinese official named Wan-Hu. In A.D. 1235, he assembled a rocket-powered chair. Forty-seven rockets were attached to the back of his chair, and two large kites were tied to his shoulders. Forty-seven assistants were recruited to set off all the explosions at once. There was a tremendous roar accompanied by billowing clouds that darkened the sky. When the smoke cleared, there was no sign of Wan-Hu and his flying chair. Only a pile of ashes marked the spot.

A reconstruction of one of William Congreve's rockets. More than 170 years later modern rocket technology has produced weapons of awesome accuracy and power.

produced twenty-four-pound missiles with a range of more than a mile. Accuracy was a problem. Fuse material had to be delicately adjusted, and there was no certainty these rockets would hit their target.

On the night of October 8, 1806, during England's war with France, the British quietly launched eighteen small oar-powered landing craft containing Congreve's new weapons. These were three-foot-long rockets equipped with liquid fuel warheads that sprayed flames from holes in their pointed nose caps. When they struck the wooden enemy ships, the battle was over.

AMAZING FACTS

Congreve's rockets were used by British ships against the United States in 1812. They inspired Francis Scott Key to write about "the rockets' red glare" in his poem that later became "The Star Spangled Banner."

9

Dreaming of Space Travel

About the turn of the twentieth century, the idea gradually emerged that rockets were the key to space travel. Working independently, three individuals developed their own ideas for heading for the Moon, which was everyone's first goal in exploring outer space.

Konstantin Tsiolkovsky was born in Russia in 1857. He was a schoolteacher who spent his spare time dreaming of space flight and working out a number of theories on paper concerning heavier-than-air flying machines.

He calculated that in order to escape Earth's gravity, speeds of seven miles per second or twenty-six thousand miles per hour would be needed, and the only way to generate such force would be to use a rocket. He was the first to write a scientific paper proving that it would be possible one day for rocket-propelled craft to travel through the vacuum of space. While Tsiolkovsky developed brilliant theories, he did not extend himself to perform practical experimental work.

In contrast to Tsiolkovsky, American Robert Hutchings Goddard did more than put figures on paper. Although his rockets never reached the high altitude required to break into Earth orbit, his work was important in developing test models that were the forerunners of space rockets to come. He experimented with different fuel propellants and fired his rockets during all weather conditions. Some of his rockets collected valuable data on atmospheric conditions. This data was used to analyze the chemical makeup of the thinning air above Earth.

In Germany, Hermann Oberth was also building rockets. Rocket propulsion for many uses was his goal. Oberth had the ability to inspire others to continue his work and theories.

Shortly before World War I (1914–1918), Oberth became interested in military weapons, but when Germany lost the war, it was forbidden to manufacture any more armaments. German scientists turned from making guns to developing rockets they

AMAZING FACTS

Konstantin Tsiolkovsky designed a passenger rocket train for the year 2017. His plans called for twenty single rockets, each with its own engine and propellants. It would be more than three hundred feet long, twelve feet in diameter, built in three layers of metal, with quartz windows — all materials chosen for their ability to withstand high temperatures. He concluded that by discarding the spent fuel tanks one after another, the required velocity could be reached to break the pull of Earth's gravity.

claimed were only for space exploration. At the same time, the country's rocket enthusiasts founded the Society for Space Travel.

The USSR, as well as Germany, was thinking about breaking the space barrier. The world was looking toward the heavens, and nothing seemed impossible.

This 1922 illustration is an artist's impression of Robert Hutchings Goddard's design for a rocket that could travel to the Moon. It would be many years before a rocket this size became a reality.

11

Robert Hutchings Goddard (1882–1945)

Robert Hutchings Goddard was born in Worcester, Massachusetts, on October 5, 1882. As a boy, he showed an aptitude for science and mathematics and his imagination led him to dream of traveling through outer space. He admitted to having been inspired by many science fiction writers of the day. It seems ironic that fiction writers caught the public fancy while the man who spent his entire life trying to make these fantasies come true was never taken seriously until after his death.

While still in high school, Goddard wrote several articles on the possibility of space flight. He suggested that the heat from radioactive materials might serve as a fuel to make interplanetary travel possible. His articles were rejected by science magazines, but his interest in all aspects of rockets never lessened. Even at home, he worked on rocket design, alarming neighbors and family — luckily, no one was hurt in these initial experiments.

Goddard in 1924 with one of his experiments, a rocket charged with gun cotton, an explosive.

After receiving his bachelor's degree, Goddard continued his graduate work in physics at Clark University. He shared, without knowing it, Tsiolkovsky's conclusions that liquid hydrogen and liquid oxygen would be an ideal fuel combination. He applied for a grant from the Smithsonian Institution in Washington, D.C., to continue his research. Modest in his proposal, he suggested that the real value of high-altitude rockets would be in collecting information about our upper atmosphere. In 1917, he was awarded the sum of $5,000.

But World War I was to change his plans, at least for the moment. Goddard was recruited to redirect his talents in developing military rockets. He invented a hand-held rocket-launching device, forerunner of the bazooka rocket mortar. When the war ended, he turned to teaching.

One important person who read of Goddard was Colonel Charles A. Lindbergh. The famous aviator was fascinated with the potential of Goddard's work to boost the speed of aircraft on take-off. Through Lindbergh's influence, Goddard was finally awarded a $50,000 grant, which helped him put his theories into practice.

In 1926, Goddard constructed and successfully tested the first rocket using liquid propellants. Looking back, it has been said that this first flight on March 16, 1926, at Auburn, Massachusetts, was a feat as important in history as that of the Wright brothers' first airplane flights at Kitty Hawk.

Goddard then moved his rocket-testing base to an isolated site not far from Roswell, New Mexico, where he, his wife, and four assistants set up their rather primitive equipment to test his rocket theories. Ever persistent, but rarely appreciated, Goddard's research framed rocket design that would eventually lift us into space.

Goddard with his first liquid fueled rocket in 1926. The flight lasted less than three seconds.

It was not until after his death on August 10, 1945, that he was fully appreciated. In 1959, two medals were presented to his widow, and one of NASA's major facilities, the Goddard Space Flight Center, was named after him. In 1960, the United States government made a cash payment of $500,000 to Mrs. Goddard in settlement for the government's use of more than two hundred of the pioneer's patents.

— Chapter 2 —
The Race Begins

A 1927 artist's impression of Max Valier's proposed solar-powered lunar base. At the time, many scientists were obsessed with ideas of space travel, but in the 1930s, rocket research turned toward producing deadly new weapons.

The race to be the first in space started well before the beginning of World War II. The first flight of a liquid-propelled rocket in Europe took place on March 14, 1931, in Breslau, Germany. Johannes Winkler's eleven-pound rocket fuelled by a methane and oxygen mixture reached an altitude of nearly one thousand feet — not much of a record, but for a new form of propellant, it could be considered a great success.

Other countries were also experimenting. In the mid-1930s, British, Soviet, Italian, Austrian, French, German, and American rocketeers joined interplanetary societies and exchanged ideas openly. It was a time of trust, a short period when scientists believed that, by pooling their research, someone might be able to design a machine that would reach magical heights.

A nine-volume encyclopedia covering every aspect of space flight was published in the Soviet Union in 1932. It included proposals for communicating with other worlds, even some wild ideas about changing the course of planets and comets.

The Soviet Union versus Germany

In 1936, the Soviets proved to be ahead in the space race, if it could be called that, by developing a sixty-five-pound rocket, eight and one-half feet long and slightly more than six inches in diameter. It reached an altitude of more than three miles. By the next year, a Russian rocket reached an altitude of three and one-half miles. The rocket weighed 213 pounds and was ten feet long and just under a foot in diameter.

That record was soon broken, and the Germans were in first place again. They were also trying to adapt rocket propulsion for other forms of transportation. A car was equipped with rockets, and tests followed on a rocket-propelled railway car. In 1935, Wernher von Braun mounted a rocket on a small aircraft.

These pioneering efforts were ahead of their time, but no one considered them very practical, so it was back to "sky rockets."

Germany Develops a Secret Weapon

In 1932, the German rocket society was without funds. A great financial depression had spread around the world forcing German scientists to seek help from the army to carry on their research. They were granted permission to use the army testing grounds at Kummersdorf near Berlin. Suddenly, a screen of secrecy was drawn. German scientists withdrew from international research meetings. News only occasionally emerged of what was going on in that country.

During this time, the German government developed an impressive military base and testing site at Peenemünde, a small fishing village on a large island in the Baltic Sea. Between 1932, when the young graduate student Wernher von Braun was working on his doctorate thesis in physics, helped by a single mechanic, and 1937, the staff grew to about eighty. Eventually, about seventeen thousand scientists, engineers, and military personnel were stationed on the island to develop their mystery weapon.

AMAZING FACTS

During the early 1930s, rocket scientist Max Valier, wanting to publicize the capabilities of rocket transportation, got together with Fritz von Opel, who manufactured sports cars and wanted publicity for his automobiles. They produced the first rocket-powered car equipped with twenty-four rockets. With Opel himself at the wheel, the car sped down the track at nearly 125 miles per hour, a record for the time.

Wernher von Braun (1912–1977)

Wernher von Braun and his two brothers grew up as members of an affluent family. Their father was minister of education and agriculture in the German High Command, but the senior von Braun had no connection with the military.

Von Braun in 1954 with a model of a V-2 rocket.

Only eighteen, von Braun had just graduated from a technical school with high honors in science when he joined Hermann Oberth's group of rocket scientists. In spite of his lack of experience, it wasn't long before his analytical ability and engineering talents were recognized. He continued his studies in physics and received his doctorate degree in April 1934.

It was only logical that the rocket group would accept government support when a fine test site was set up at Peenemünde. In return, the scientists were required to focus their entire research on rockets for military use. The army's interest in von Braun's ability to develop military applications for rockets clashed with von Braun's main interest — building a machine to break the bonds of Earth's gravity.

Early in his career that enthusiasm led to von Braun's arrest. The German Gestapo (security police) thought he spent too much time working on plans for space travel and not enough time developing rockets as a military weapon. He was accused of sabotage. He was released only when General Dornberger, who was head of the project, explained to Hitler that this young man working on the big rocket was indispensable to the program.

When reports came back to Germany that the V-2 rockets he had designed worked perfectly, von Braun was quoted as saying to a friend that the only trouble was that they had landed on the wrong planet. He never doubted that space flight would be possible during his lifetime.

As Germany foundered, von Braun made a critical decision. He had no intention of destroying the years of work that had seen such progress in rocket science. The United States seemed the next logical great power to continue the work.

When arrangements were finally made at the time of surrender for von Braun and a select few of his staff to come to America, he did not hesitate to accept, even though it meant leaving his family behind for the first few months.

The German team was first sent to New Mexico, the rocket-proving grounds where Goddard had once set up his test site. They stayed there until 1950, when the Korean War began. Then they were transferred to Redstone Arsenal in Alabama to build a long-range nuclear missile.

A rocket of the same basic design as the Redstone missile carried the United States into the space race with the Soviet Union. It powered both *Explorer I*, launched in January 1958, and the first U.S. piloted flight three years later.

By then, von Braun's engineering skills and visionary leadership had made him a hero to his adopted country. Yet he never lost sight of his goal. Asked what it would take to build a rocket capable of reaching the Moon, he answered simply, "The will to do it."

Made head of Redstone's new Marshall Space Flight Center, von Braun put that will to work on the biggest job of his career, building the massive Saturn V rocket for Project Apollo. In July 1969, *Apollo 11* fulfilled not only a U.S. pledge but von Braun's own lifelong dream to put a man on the Moon.

He still had grand plans for the future — landing a man on Mars before the end of the 1980s and the development of bases on the Moon. None of these plans were approved by a cost-conscious Congress.

Von Braun announced his retirement from NASA in 1972 and accepted a position in private industry. He died of cancer in 1977 but not before being awarded the National Medal of Science by President Gerald Ford.

The launch of Apollo 11 *atop a Saturn V rocket was the culmination of von Braun's work through the 1950s and 1960s. Here, he opens an exhibition about the* Apollo 11 *mission.*

The German army wanted a long-range missile, capable of flying 150 to perhaps 200 miles with a one-ton explosive charge. The rocket had to be compact enough to be transported by railway or truck so that launch sites could be kept secret.

The V-2 and the Blitz

The result of all this clandestine effort was the V-2 rocket. It was small by comparison to today's rockets, but it made history as the prototype of rockets to come. It achieved its great thrust by burning a mixture of liquid oxygen and alcohol at a rate of about one ton every seven seconds. Once launched, the V-2 was a formidable weapon that could destroy whole city blocks.

And that's what it was used for. Germany was at war with Britain, and London was the main target. Air raid sirens warning of V-2s overhead brought terror, but the British reacted with bravery, not defeat. They learned to head for air raid shelters, and fire brigades managed to contain the worst of the V-2 firestorms.

Fortunately for London and the Allied forces, the V-2 came too late in the war to change its outcome. But German rocket scientists and engineers had already laid plans for advanced missiles capable of crossing the Atlantic Ocean and landing in America.

German V-2 rocket in a museum. In 1943, worried at the course World War II was taking, Hitler demanded round-the-clock production of this new weapon.

The Fall of Germany

In late January of 1945, when it had become apparent that the German Third Reich was collapsing, Wernher von Braun met secretly with his top staff members to decide whether they should remain at Peenemünde and surrender to the advancing Russian army or move south and contact American Allied forces. Hitler had vowed that all models of his prize weapon and related documents would be destroyed. It was rumored that he might plan to exterminate the staff that could repeat this research.

The scientists were ordered to move into an empty army camp in southern Germany. Von Braun sent his English-speaking brother, Magnus von Braun, to try to contact the nearby American Forty-fourth Infantry Division.

At first, the Americans did not realize what a treasure was being offered. If it had not been for American Colonel Gervais Trichel, who knew of the underground V-2 plant at Nordhausen, the personnel and all sample prototypes would have either been destroyed by the Germans or captured by other Allied divisions. A move was made to list the key German rocket scientists to be interrogated and offered a chance to come to the United States. On July 19, 1945, the project was christened "Operation Paperclip."

The Americans moved their troops in quickly. When they captured the huge underground rocket factory, they found it almost completely intact. This section of Germany was soon to be turned over to the Russians as a result of the Yalta agreement. Before the deadline was reached, they loaded 341 freight cars with about a hundred V-2 ballistic missiles. At Antwerp, the equipment was loaded onto ships and transported to New Orleans and later to the New Mexico desert.

Von Braun and 127 of his associates were offered one-year contracts to come to the United States to work for the Army Ordinance Corps. All of them accepted. The next steps in rocketry taken by the United States would be led by these scientists and others like them.

AMAZING FACTS

The Germans built an entire underground factory to manufacture the V-2 rocket. It was built into a mountain to hide it from the Allies. Fourteen tons of documents outlining all the research for the rocket were hidden in an abandoned mine tunnel. They were retrieved by American troops at the end of the war.

— Chapter 3 —
Rockets Get Bigger

The story of rockets in the postwar era is a story of competition between two great powers, the United States and the USSR. Each power was afraid the other was outpacing it in the field of deadly weapons.

In the United States, each of the military divisions — Army, Air Force, and Navy with help from the Marines — was developing its own classification of weapons. The Air Force was busy developing the Snark and Matador rockets. Snark was capable of traveling five thousand to seven thousand miles. It weighed fifty thousand pounds, was powered by a turbojet engine, and was boosted to operational speed by two thirty-three thousand-pound solid-fuel rockets. The Matador was smaller with a shorter range.

Rockets Go Farther

Finally, the U.S. decided to concentrate on a true intercontinental ballistic missile (ICBM) that could travel thousands of miles along arcs that took them out into space. *Ballistic missile* means any missile that is powered at takeoff by a rocket engine but becomes a free-falling object as it reaches its target. In other words, it's shot into the upper atmosphere with a tremendous rocket boost, but when it reaches the peak of its flight, gravity and air resistance shape its course. Whether it hits a target accurately depends on complicated timing and the angle of the rocket when it leaves the launch site. What the Army designed was an impressive vehicle boosted into the air by three liquid-propellant rocket engines, capable of traveling to its target at three times the speed of sound.

But during the course of budgeting future armament programs, the Navaho project, as it was called, was put on hold. Part of the problem lay in camouflaging the launch sites of these huge ICBM rockets; they would make an easy target for an enemy to attack. Polaris rockets that could be fired at sea from submarines or ships were one answer. Another solution was the Minuteman rocket stored indefinitely in huge underground silos. Only rock-

A U.S. Air Force Atlas intercontinental ballistic missile, covered in ice, lifts off from Cape Canaveral, Florida. German and American scientists had joined together to develop the V-2 into the Atlas series.

ets with solid propellants could be stored in this way because their fuel would not have to be loaded just before launch as with other systems. They could be fired almost instantly to targets programmed into their guidance systems. This is about as close to push-button warfare as was ever devised.

The Americans felt rather secure, thinking that their weapons were more accurate and more numerous than the Soviets'. Nuclear warheads were now smaller than at first design. Americans felt that a smaller rocket would do as much damage as giants with much less powerful warheads. So they did not design the real giants of space rockets that the Soviets had started to test. Although peace had been declared after World War II, the main thrust of rocket research was still aimed at military preparedness and defense.

Dr. Ernst Stuhlinger

One of the earlier space pioneers was Dr. Ernst Stuhlinger, director of science at NASA's Marshall Space Flight Center. He was educated in Germany, and as a member of a research group studying nuclear physics, Dr. Stuhlinger worked for seven years with Dr. Hans Geiger, developer of the Geiger counter to monitor radiation.

Stuhlinger served in the German Army before he transferred to the Rocket Development and Test Center near Peenemünde,

Germany. He was one of the scientists who accompanied Wernher von Braun to the United States after World War II, becoming a U.S. citizen in 1955.

Under Stuhlinger's direction, early planning for lunar exploration began. Work in his laboratory included preliminary studies for a large space telescope, which was installed in the space lab vehicle. Some of these early designs were incorporated in the Hubble Space Telescope, which was launched in 1990 from the space shuttle. So, thanks to Stuhlinger, modern astronomers can, for the first time, view the universe outside the blanket of cosmic dust wrapped around our own planet. The Hubble Space Telescope will be in service for at least twenty more years — longer if NASA is able to service any future problems the telescope may develop.

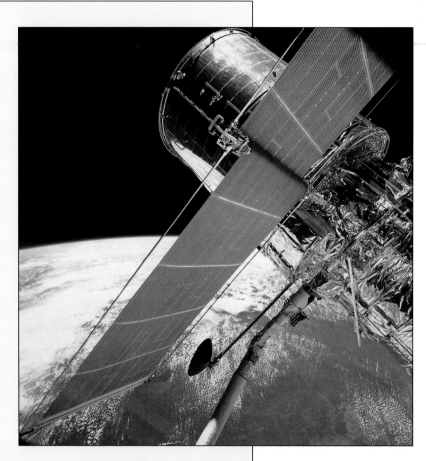

Stuhlinger's work was useful in the design of the Hubble Space Telescope, here being deployed by the space shuttle Discovery in 1990. It is still attached to the shuttle by the remote manipulator arm at the bottom of the picture. In the foreground, a solar panel is unfurling.

Stuhlinger has gained scientific recognition in the United States and abroad for his studies of electric propulsion systems for space vehicles. In sharp contrast to gigantic starship power plants, electric propulsion systems are extremely small, weighing a thousand times less than most other propulsion systems. Their thrust is extremely low, coming in pulses of power, but the "push" generated is sufficient in the vacuum and near-zero gravity of space to make them valuable for interplanetary travel. Their fuel consumption is minimal, and the weight saved on such a vehicle makes them extremely useful.

Dr. Stuhlinger has written a number of books and dozens of articles on nuclear and space physics, electric and nuclear rocket propulsion, on space vehicles, satellites, astronomy, and what is in store for the future of space flight. He has been awarded many honors for his work.

An artist's impression, from a magazine of the time, of the dog Laika orbiting the Earth in Sputnik 2. Scientists were eager to find out how living organisms coped with life in space.

AMAZING FACTS

The USSR's first lunar probe took photographs of the far side of the Moon for the first time on October 4, 1959.

Soviet Success

All these American accomplishments faded when news broke that on October 4, 1957, the USSR had fired the world's first carrier rocket to place an artificial satellite in orbit. The satellite, *Sputnik*, weighed 184 pounds. A very faint spot in the heavens, it was the first artificial object ever to orbit the Earth, circling the planet every one and one-half hours. Newspapers gave exact times when people could spot the object with binoculars. Humans had broken the bounds of gravity. Now almost anything seemed possible.

The Soviets quickly followed this dramatic success with another. *Sputnik 2* launched less than a month later, carried a dog named Laika and weighed as much as 1,120 pounds.

In contrast, America's record in space was a modest one. On January 31, 1958, *Explorer I* was launched. It was about the size of a basketball and weighed 10.5 pounds. On March 17, 1958, *Vanguard I*, the first satellite to incorporate solar cells, was launched. It is still in orbit today.

Now, the Soviets, with their heavier rockets, were ahead in the space race. All branches of the U.S. military would have to pool their resources to compete. So President Dwight D. Eisenhower established the National Aeronautics and Space Administration (NASA) in April 1958. NASA started as a name only but grew by absorption, taking over the administration of the Army-owned Jet Propulsion Lab in California, the Air Force's Upper Atmosphere Sounding Group, and finally von Braun's group of scientists in Huntsville, Alabama.

Chapter 4 —
How Rockets Work

Von Braun realized that the ICBM-based carrier rockets then in production were not powerful enough for piloted missions in Earth's orbit, but that bigger rockets could be built using existing technology. However, certain mathematical equations had to be followed. The amount of thrust (force) produced by a rocket engine will be determined by the mass of rocket fuel that is burned and how fast the resulting gas escapes the rocket.

Rockets today operate with either solid or liquid propellants. The word propellant does not simply mean fuel but rather both fuel and oxidizer (oxygen). For the fuel to burn, an oxidizer must be present. Jet engines draw oxygen from the air, but in outer space there is no air, so rockets must carry their own oxygen. When the propellant is ignited, gases expand in a small trapped space and must find an escape.

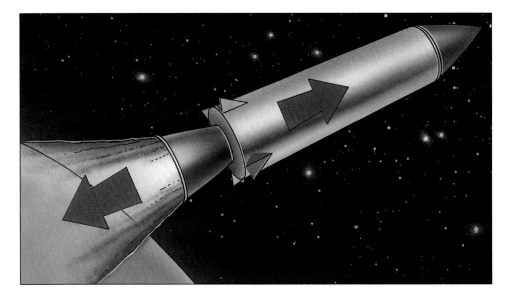

The explosive power of the hot gases escaping the rear of a rocket causes an equal reaction in the opposite direction. This reaction is the thrust or forward force that sends the rocket upwards.

A U.S. Air Force Delta 3920 rocket sits on the launch pad. Delta rockets have been used to launch many kinds of satellites into space. They may have two or three stages, with up to nine solid-propellant strap-on boosters.

The nozzle of a solid propellant rocket is an opening at the back of the rocket that permits the hot expanding gases to escape. The narrow part of the nozzle is the throat. Just beyond the throat is the exit cone. The throat cuts down the size of the opening to increase the speed of the gases as they escape. Turn on a garden hose and see how much further a stream of water can spray when the nozzle opening is slightly closed by your thumb.

The sides of the combustion chamber of a rocket prevent the gases from escaping sideways. The only opening to the outside is the nozzle. These hot gases have mass, and this mass can only escape through the rocket's nozzle at high velocities. If the chamber were sealed, all these pressures would be balanced, and the rocket would not move. The gases are allowed to escape at high speed through the nozzle, causing an imbalance of pressure in the chamber. In the rocket, the escaping exhaust gases are the action, and the forward pressure, or thrust, is the reaction, so the rocket moves forward.

Three Types of Propellant

Solid propellants are dry to the touch and contain both fuel and oxidizer. This is the simplest type of rocket fuel. All that is needed is a way to ignite the core of the rocket. With the Chinese fiery arrows, a fuse was lit by a torch. An electrical current is far safer. There are other more complicated ways to start the reaction and engineers are always looking for improvements.

A rocket using a solid propellant cannot be shut off until its fuel has been consumed, but it has the advantage of always being ready for launch. Solid propellants are stable and easily stored.

The total thrust is the greatest at takeoff and gradually decreases as the material burns away.

The space shuttle lifts off using the largest solid-propellant rocket motors ever built and flown. Each reusable booster contains 1.1 million pounds of propellant in the form of a chemical mixture held together by a hard rubbery substance with the consistency of a pencil eraser.

A rocket using a liquid propellant has a much more complicated engine with a series of pumps and gauges to mix the fuel. There are three kinds of liquid propellant in use today.

Petroleum propellant is a type of kerosene similar to that burned in heaters and lamps, though rocket petroleum is highly refined. It was used to power the first stages of many of the

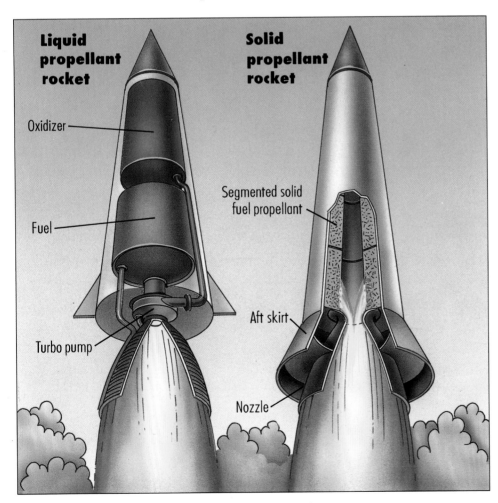

Liquid propellant rocket

Oxidizer

Fuel

Turbo pump

Solid propellant rocket

Segmented solid fuel propellant

Aft skirt

Nozzle

The diagram shows two types of propellants in use today. The space shuttle uses both on its journey out of Earth's atmosphere. Liquid propellant rockets use liquid hydrogen as fuel and liquid oxygen as oxidizer. Solid propellant rockets burn a mixture of fuel and oxidizer in solid form.

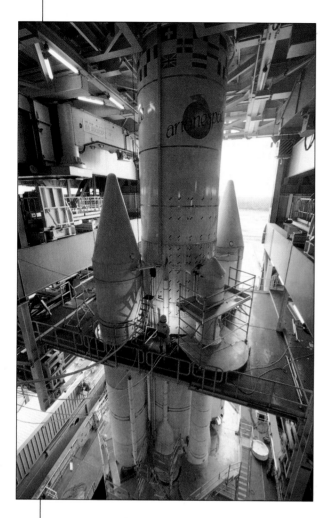

An Ariane 4 rocket is fueled in French Guiana. The technician fueling the rocket on the platform in the center is wearing an airtight suit because hypergolic fuels are extremely toxic. All the people watching the launch wear gas masks in case an accident occurs.

earlier types of rockets, but it delivers a thrust considerably less than that of cryogenic fuels.

That strange word, *cryogenic*, comes from a Greek word meaning "ice cold." Oxygen is usually thought of as a gas, but it turns into a liquid state at temperatures of minus 298° Fahrenheit (minus 183° Celsius). Hydrogen becomes a liquid at temperatures of minus 423° Fahrenheit (minus 253° Celsius).

If either oxygen or hydrogen were used as a gas, it would require extremely large tanks to store them aboard a rocket. Cooling and compressing the gases into liquids increase their density and make it possible to store them in much smaller compartments. The main problem is the necessity to keep them at these very cold temperatures to prevent them returning to gases. The fuel cells in the orbiter of the space shuttle use this fuel because liquid hydrogen and liquid oxygen burn cleanly, leaving a byproduct of water vapor, which can be reused as water.

The third type of propellant is called hypergolic. These fuels and oxidizers need no ignition system because they ignite on contact with each other. This easy start and restart capability makes them useful for both piloted and unpiloted spacecraft. They are also easy to store and don't require such extreme temperatures as for cryogenic fuels.

Weight Is a Problem

The correct propellant for rockets was just one of the many problems that faced early rocket enthusiasts. Controlling the thrust of an engine is also very important in launching rockets into orbit. Too much thrust or thrust at the wrong time can cause a rocket to go into the wrong orbit and perhaps even cause it to fall back to Earth. Today, a computer in the rocket's guidance system controls the amount of thrust needed by regulating how fast the propellant flows.

The reason it has taken so much time in research to find just the right propellant for a rocket's engine is that the mass of the fuel is such a large proportion of the total mass. As a basic

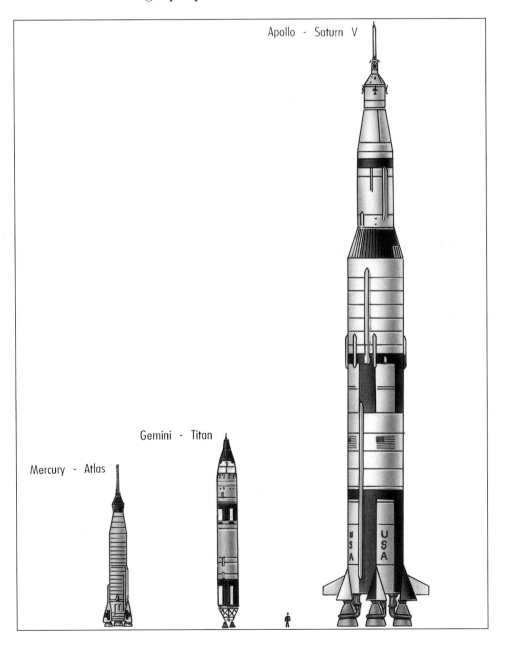

Apollo - Saturn V

Gemini - Titan

Mercury - Atlas

Rockets became larger during the 1960s as NASA planned a Moon landing. The Mercury capsule, launched by an Atlas rocket, carried one man into Earth's orbit. The Gemini capsule allowed two people to carry out maneuvers in space. The Apollo 11 spacecraft needed the massive Saturn V rocket to lift three astronauts and all their equipment away from the pull of Earth's gravity on its journey to the Moon.

Rollout of a Saturn IB rocket on a transporter from the assembly building to its launch site at the Kennedy Space Center, Florida. The launch takes place at a distance from the center and the flight takes the rocket out over the ocean, minimizing damage in case of an accident.

principle of rocket flight, the engine must produce a thrust that is greater than the total mass of the vehicle. The mass of a rocket must be trimmed to just the bare essentials.

For an ideal rocket, 91 percent of the total mass should be taken up as propellants, 3 percent should be tanks, engines, and other hardware, which leaves only 6 percent for the payload of instruments and humans it carries into space.

Large rockets able to carry vehicles into space have enormous weight problems. One solution has been to send up rockets built in stages. When the first stage of a rocket has exhausted its fuel, the empty casing is dropped off, and the lighter load that remains can pick up speed.

Rockets are able to move in the vacuum of space even though there is no air for them to push against. In fact, the thrust of a rocket is more efficient when there is no atmosphere to hinder the escaping gas.

Chapter 5
To the Moon and Back

The space race continued in earnest. The Soviets took advantage of their superior ability in lifting heavy loads and, on September 12, 1959, aimed a rocket at the Moon. It landed precisely on target, but the impact on landing damaged its instruments, so no information was sent back to Earth. It was still an impressive accomplishment and caused Americans to wonder why their own space program was lagging behind.

From May 1960 to March 1961, the Americans launched a series of five satellites that were the forerunners of piloted spacecraft, since they carried either live organisms or mannequins that were designed for recovery. Liquid-fueled retrorockets were tested on two of the satellites. A retrorocket is a small rocket engine that is mounted on a larger rocket or spacecraft. Its nozzle faces in the opposite direction to the nozzle on the larger rocket. It therefore provides reverse thrust, a braking force used to slow down the carrier vehicle when coming in for a landing.

On April 12, 1961, more news came from the Soviet Union. Vostok, a 125-foot tall rocket, had lifted Yuri Gagarin, the first man in space, into orbit. The

A contemporary artist's impression of the Soviet Luna 2 *crash-landing on the Moon in 1959. At the time, people had little idea what the Moon's surface was like or how the Earth would appear from space.*

Il primo razzo sulla Luna
(Disegno di Walter Molino; vedi pagina 4)

The U.S.'s first piloted orbital space flight blasts off from Cape Canaveral in February 1962. The Atlas rocket carried John Glenn into orbit in a capsule that was only slightly bigger than he was.

USSR seemed to be winning the space race with its large booster rockets, but the United States took up the challenge. On May 1, 1961, President John F. Kennedy declared a national space flight goal: a piloted Moon landing before the end of the decade.

Four days later, Alan Shepard was shot aloft atop a Redstone 2 rocket — America's first attempt to put a man into space. Not planned as an orbital flight, his journey was to last only fifteen minutes. But he was able to explore many of the unknowns of space travel, questions that space chimps could not — and Russians would not — answer. There was also the crucial test to see if the parachute landing apparatus would bring him in for a safe splashdown. Shepard returned a hero and dispelled the fears of many that the pressures of space flight might somehow harm the brains of humans.

It was not until February 20 of the following year that John Glenn became America's first astronaut to circle the Earth. His flight took him on three orbits of the Earth, but after the first orbit, a malfunction occurred in the automatic control system. By being able to take charge of the craft, Glenn made a strong case for the need to have an astronaut aboard a spacecraft to take care of any unexpected emergencies.

Over the next three years, record after record was broken with longer flights and more complex tasks performed each mission.

On June 3, 1965, Edward White became the first American to don a pressurized suit to walk in space outside a spacecraft.

Dress Rehearsal

Before a Moon landing could be scheduled, another major project to be accomplished was the meeting of two spacecraft in flight. It had always been planned that a small landing craft would be used when touching down on the Moon. After the initial exploration was finished, the landing craft would have to return to the larger vehicle for the trip back to Earth.

The dress rehearsal for such a meeting took place in December 1965, as the *Gemini 7* spacecraft caught up with *Gemini 6*

Gemini 6 *and* 7 *approach each other. Gemini capsules held two people, although three astronauts would be needed for a Moon landing.*

Astronauts practiced many maneuvers in space before the first successful Moon landing. Here, David Scott leaves the command module of Apollo 9. These modules were far bigger than the Mercury and Gemini modules that preceded them because they had to contain more supplies and equipment.

already in space. Although no docking maneuvers were attempted this time, the two spacecraft flew side by side, sometimes no more than a foot apart.

Now everyone was waiting for the main event, the landing of a man on the Moon. The Moon's surface had been mapped, equipment tested. All promises made now by the president of the United States and NASA had to be kept.

"A Giant Step"

On July 16, 1969, *Apollo 11* was ready on the launch pad at Cape Canaveral. It towered 353 feet into the sky. Hundreds of people had assembled long before the 9:30 takeoff time. Ignition was finally set. Slowly, the huge rocket shook loose the half a ton of ice that had built up on the side of the second stage tank holding the supercold liquid propellant. As the acceleration continued, the rocket lifted its ponderous weight into the air with a trail of smoke that penciled across the sky.

Four days later, the whole world watched anxiously as astronaut Neil Armstrong set his bulkily-clad foot on lunar soil and

The launch of Apollo 11 from the Kennedy Space Center in July 1969. The Saturn V rocket used to power the flight was discarded in sections as the fuel was used up, leaving the command module, with the lunar module inside, to continue the journey to the Moon.

spoke the famous words, "That's one small step for a man, one giant step for mankind."

He and his teammate Buzz Aldrin took a few tentative steps away from their landing craft, and then, gaining confidence, they hopped around like playful kids, experiencing for the first time the weak lunar gravity. They stayed on the Moon's surface for twenty and one-half hours before returning to the *Eagle*, the landing craft that would take them back to rejoin Mike Collins, the pilot in the orbiting command module *Columbia*.

Other astronauts were now waiting in line for a chance to explore the Moon's surface. Years of training had put them at the top of the list for this once-in-a-lifetime experience.

From Research to Near-Tragedy

With the first lunar landing accomplished, the thrust of the Apollo program shifted from pioneering space travel to scientific research. In November 1969, a second team of astronauts set up a complicated package of experiments, powered by a small nuclear generator, to measure moonquakes, the Moon's magnetic field, and other phenomena that had never been studied. They stayed nearly three times as long as the *Apollo 11* crew and collected a vast store of rocks that would reveal much about lunar history.

Apollo 13 lifted off on April 11, 1970, and almost came to grief when an oxygen tank in the service module exploded en route to the Moon. The crew — mission commander James Lovell, command-module pilot Jack Swigert, and lunar-module pilot Fred Haise — stayed alive through their own quick thinking and the incredible teamwork of the ground crews back in Houston.

With only fifteen minutes before their last fuel cell went out, all unnecessary systems were closed down. The important task was to put the craft back on course to take them home. This meant swinging around the far side of the Moon before the descent pattern could head them back to Earth.

(Opposite) Buzz Aldrin takes his first step onto the lunar surface. When astronauts drilled holes in the Moon's surface they discovered that beneath the top layer of powdered dust was a much firmer layer than had been expected.

AMAZING FACTS

Alan Shepard, the first American man in space, had been sidelined from active duty because of ear problems until he was assigned to the *Apollo 14* mission. Extracting two golf balls that he had smuggled into his space suit, he used an implement from his tool cart to execute what he called a sand trap shot, the first golf shot ever made on the lunar surface.

Saverio Morea

In spite of his impressive title as one of the directors of the Marshall Space Flight Center in Huntsville, Alabama, Saverio Morea is affectionately known as Sonny to his coworkers. That is a name that has followed him since his birth in 1932 in Queens, New York.

Morea can't remember a time when he wasn't thinking of outer space. He earned his pilot license at age fourteen, long before he was permitted behind the wheel of his father's car. Even today, if he has any spare time, he enjoys being a flight instructor.

He graduated from Brooklyn Technical High School in 1950, where he participated in the aeronautical engineering program. He received a bachelor of mechanical engineering degree in 1954 from City College in New York.

Morea began his professional career in 1954 as an engineer working in the aerophysics department of North American Aviation (now Rockwell) on the Navaho missile program. In 1955, he was assigned to Dr. Wernher von Braun's group of scientists and engineers as a lieutenant, where he spent his military assignment working on the guidance and control systems of the Redstone missile. After resuming civilian status, Morea switched to his field of choice, working on propulsion systems for the Jupiter and later the Saturn rockets.

In 1969, he was appointed project manager for the development of the Lunar Roving Vehicle. This was the first powered "car" to be driven on the Moon. It looked like a stripped-down version of a dune buggy with wide tires and webbed seats for two. It was crammed with scientific instruments and an umbrella-like receiving system for capturing radio waves.

Astronauts David Scott and Jim Erwin renamed it their "Bucking Bronco" as they set off on a series of eight-mile sweeps that took them through eighteen miles of lunar highlands. They ventured to the rim of the Hadley Rille, a twelve hundred-foot deep canyon that geologists believe was scoured early in lunar history by fast flowing molten lava. One hundred and seventy-five pounds of Moon rock were gathered, including one piece that later proved to be more than four billion years old, older than any rocks found on Earth, almost as old as the solar system. It was dubbed the "Genesis Rock."

Two more landings with the Rover were made. Although it was the astronauts we watched on television, it was the work of Saverio Morea and his team who made it all possible, and for this, Morea was given the NASA Exceptional Service Medal for the second time in his career. The first award was for his contributions to the *Apollo 11* mission in the field of propulsion development and management.

While Saverio Morea never accomplished a Moon landing himself, he was there in spirit and on constant monitor watch every minute of space time. For relaxation, he flies as high as a conventional civilian airplane will take him. The sky hardly seems to limit his soaring imagination.

The Lunar Roving Vehicle was ten feet long and eight feet wide. It could be folded within the lunar module.

What remains of the Apollo 11 command module lands in the sea. It was built to withstand great heat as it reentered the Earth's atmosphere. The astronauts inside the floating vehicle had to wait for rescue craft to locate them.

The astronauts arrived home safely, disappointed to have missed a landing on the Moon, but everyone realized that much had been learned about rigging up backup systems. It also proved that America's astronauts were able to work under the most frightening stress.

Four other lunar missions were accomplished. In all, a dozen astronauts had a chance to explore the surface of our nearest neighbor. There were many more on Earth who played important roles in the success of these missions.

— Chapter 6 —
Laboratory in the Sky

Whof plans
were in the making. The next step was to send a full-scale laboratory into orbit that could be used for long periods by astronauts. *Skylab* was the result, but it had a disastrous beginning.

The Skylab *space station in Earth orbit. It was launched by a Saturn V rocket and orbited the Earth at an altitude of about 310 miles. Skylab contained an astronomical observatory, and thousands of photos were taken of Earth and the Sun.*

Little more than a minute after liftoff on May 12, 1973, the *Skylab*'s thermal shield broke away, tearing with it one of the winglike solar cell panels that was to help power the $2.5 billion-dollar lab. Without the wraparound shield, the space station was being scorched by the intense rays of the Sun.

Mission commander Pete Conrad, pilot Paul Weitz, and science pilot Joseph Kerwin learned the bad news the night before their own launch was to take them to their new headquarters in the sky. Now their main mission was to salvage the long-awaited science laboratory. Solving the problem required the cooperation of ground crews and engineers as well as the expert on-site work of Pete Conrad and Joseph Kerwin.

To gain some time until a more permanent solution could be found, Mission Control at Houston fired the small thruster rockets that ringed the station, to tilt the damaged area away from the Sun. When the astronauts finally arrived at the scene, they donned their pressurized space suits and tried to pry the damaged panel into place. Unable to do this on the first try, they rigged up a sun shield, a twenty-two by twenty-four-foot rectangular parasol attached to a ten-foot pole, which had been made by workers at Mission Control hours before the astronauts were sent into space.

This brought the temperature in the *Skylab* down to acceptable limits. Finally, the solar panel was freed, and the astronaut scientists started on the work that had been previously planned.

Adjusting to Space

The workshop was forty-eight feet high, crammed with equipment to study both the Earth below them and the sky above. But the most important experiments were conducted on the astronauts themselves. Could humans endure zero gravity for long periods of time? The astronauts had all suffered from queasy stomach distress upon their arrival in space. It had taken two or three days for them to adjust to their new environment.

AMAZING FACTS

The first Earth surveys from *Skylab* uncovered new deposits of oil, ore, and water that no one on Earth had been able to discover.

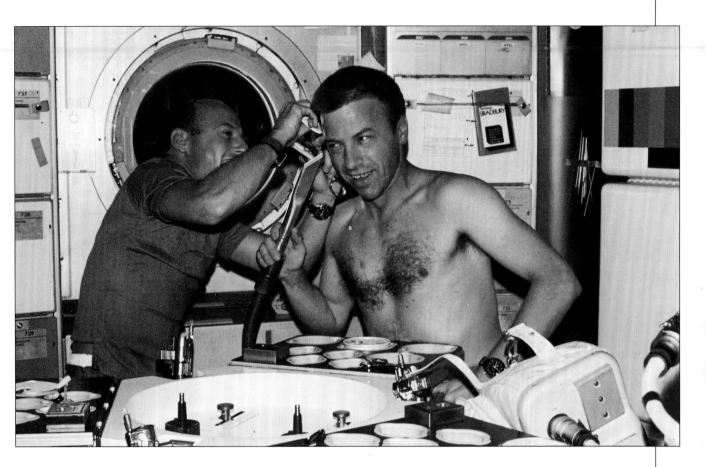

In the photos they sent back to Earth, it looked like fun to be floating around their work quarters, but it took a bit of adjusting to know how to anchor themselves when they wanted to stay in one place. The soles of their shoes were fitted with soft cleats. The floors and ceilings of the workshop were open grids into which the floating astronauts could hook their shoes.

Taking a shower wasn't easy either. Only a small quantity of fine mist was dispensed inside a canvas enclosure, and this had to be sucked away quickly to stop it floating throughout the cabin.

Food came in tubes or in sticky pouches, but every calorie had been counted to keep the astronauts in good shape. They exercised on a regular schedule. A type of treadmill and stationary bicycle had been provided. Their days were kept full.

The first crew spent twenty-eight days in space. It had not been a cruise without hardship. All had lost weight and especially

Astronauts shaving in the Skylab crew quarters. Skylab was occupied by three successive teams of three astronauts. They provided much-needed information about how human bodies react to spending weeks and months in space.

leg muscle. All had temporarily grown an inch taller because without the weight of gravity, their spinal columns had stretched. Their hearts had shrunk about 3 percent and raced when required to pump on Earth, but within a few days of their return, the astronauts' complaints disappeared.

Skylab kept going for five more years, but as its orbit dropped closer to Earth, it eventually broke up as it plummeted through the Earth's atmosphere. Luckily, the larger pieces scattered over uninhabited ocean and the Australian desert. It was a disappointing end, but a great deal had been learned.

A Joint Effort

Both the USSR and the United States had been making routine journeys into space, but little information had been exchanged. Now, it was felt that a cooperative venture would benefit both countries. The crew of a Russian Soyuz spacecraft and the crew of an Apollo mission would dock in space.

A common docking system had to be designed, flight techniques and controls coordinated. Flight crews exchanged training sessions between NASA's Houston center and the Soviets' Star City. On July 15, 1975, the mission was accomplished, docking took place, hatches were opened, and the world watched on television for the "handshake in space."

Trucking Service in Space

The cost of these spectacular journeys in space was enormous. NASA

A Soviet Soyuz spacecraft is photographed by Apollo astronauts during their meeting in space. Soyuz was designed for linkups with the Soviet Salyut orbital space station, and it was used many times between 1967 and 1981.

had long hoped for a reusable space vehicle, a hybrid designed to take off like a rocket, maneuver like a spaceship, and glide to Earth for a landing like a commercial airliner. Early rocket scientists, Wernher von Braun among them, had always planned on a reusable spacecraft.

The space shuttle was the ultimate answer. It was built with a large enough cargo bay to carry satellites to be put in orbit or experimental equipment that could be encased in aluminum canisters. These "getaway specials," as they were called, were simply turned off and on in orbit by a member of the crew. More complicated experiments would require hands-on work by mission specialists.

Who Would Fly These Missions?

NASA began recruiting a new generation of astronauts, scientists, and medical personnel, as well as pilots whose background was specifically in aviation. It took a very special kind of person to fill all NASA's requirements. Of course, they had to be in fine physical and mental condition and were expected to be knowledgeable, experts really, in at least one form of science. But after they were selected, their real education began.

NASA wanted someone who had a broad range of interests. Physicians who were recruited were given lessons in astronomy. Physicists were sent on courses in the fundamentals of medicine to make them able to handle health emergencies in outer space. Women as well as men were recruited, and the list of their accomplishments is long.

Astronauts on a space shuttle mission service the Hubble Space Telescope in December, 1993. They are replacing the original wide field and planetary camera with a new version that allows for a fault in the telescope's main mirror.

Bonnie Dunbar

Bonnie Dunbar was one of the new generation of astronauts recruited to fly the shuttle, bright and eager to learn new subjects. She explains her early interest in space travel: "I was part of the 1949 baby boom that came along some time before *Sputnik* was launched. I was the oldest of four kids, and we were very isolated from the nearest town."

A bookworm, she grew up reading a lot of science fiction. She was a good student in both science and literature, but it was a high school physics teacher who persuaded her to major in engineering.

"I considered MIT (Massachusetts Institute of Technology), but it was too expensive, and I also thought of Cal Tech (California Institute of Technology), until someone sent me a very nice letter telling me they didn't have any coeducational dormitories, which was another way of telling me they weren't academically coeducational at the time."

Bonnie Dunbar with fellow astronaut Norman E. Thagard at the Gagarin Cosmonaut Training Center, near Moscow, Russia, in 1994. She was the back-up to Thagard for a three-month tour of duty on the Russian Mir *space station.*

Fate seems to have taken a hand in Dunbar's decision to enroll at the University of Washington. The school had just been given the job of developing the heat shield for the space shuttle. Dunbar was in on the earliest research that produced the ceramic tiles that were used to protect *Columbia*, the first shuttle, from the searing heat of reentry into the Earth's atmosphere.

People still confuse her technical expertise and her degree as a ceramic engineer with the act of making clay pots. Dunbar doesn't bother to tell them her master's thesis was in the field of mechanics and kinetics of ionic diffusion in sodium beta-alumins.

Space shuttle Columbia *in production at the Rockwell factory in California. The olive green areas on the fuselage and wing are bare metal, awaiting the fitting of the last black (high temperature) and white (low temperature) thermal insulation tiles. The oval holes around the nose section are the exhausts for the orbital maneuvering thrusters. These are small rockets that allow the shuttle to change direction.*

She was a bit of a dreamer and hoped some day to fly in space, but "when you go to school and pick out a major, you don't say, 'I'm going to be an astronaut.' They'd think you were absolutely bonkers."

Dunbar didn't sit around idly waiting for NASA to call. By 1975, she was working for Rockwell International, helping to set up production facilities for the ceramic tiles to be used on the shuttle. She continued to deluge NASA with questions as to when they might be hiring women astronauts. When the call went out in 1978, she was one of the first to apply. She didn't make it on the first try, but when she tried again in 1980, she was accepted. "I just moved my office from one side of the building to another," she says with a laugh.

Bonnie Dunbar has flown on the shuttle more than once. She's now hoping that the planned space station *Freedom* (see page 51) will be completed in time for her to have the opportunity to spend more time in space.

Space shuttle Discovery *is towed to the vehicle assembly building, where it will be connected to the solid-fuel rocket boosters and the external fuel tank. The orbiter's own fuel tanks are in the two lumps on the top. The dark-colored areas on the nose and leading wing edges are made of a material even more heat-resistant than the ceramic tiles that cover the rest of the shuttle.*

The Space Shuttle Fleet

Six orbiters, the flying part of the space shuttle, have been built and flown. *Enterprise* was flown only within Earth's atmosphere, to practice shuttle approach and landing tests during 1977. It is now in storage but will be on display when a new annex is built to the Air and Space Museum in Washington, D.C.

Columbia flew the first five shuttle missions, beginning in April 1981. *Challenger* became the second operational shuttle, but it was lost in a tragic accident that happened just after its launch on January 28, 1986. All seven of its crew perished, including Christa McAuliffe, the first private citizen to ride the shuttle. She had been chosen from thousands of applicants in a program to put a teacher into space. Suddenly, the entire space program came to a halt, while NASA tried to put in every possible safety device imaginable.

Discovery made its first flight in August 1984, and *Atlantis* followed in October 1985. *Endeavour*, built to replace *Challenger*, made its debut in May 1992 with a dramatic mission that featured the rescue of a stranded commercial communications satellite.

The Shuttle's Engine

The space shuttle's main engine is the most advanced liquid-fueled rocket engine ever built. Three main engines are mounted on the orbiter aft (tail end) fuselage in a triangular pattern. The engines are spaced so that they are movable during flight and are used to steer the shuttle vehicle as well as provide thrust for launch along with the two solid rocket boosters.

Fuel for the engines — liquid hydrogen and liquid oxygen — is contained in the external belly tank, the largest element of the shuttle. Fuel is supplied from the tank at a rate of about forty-seven thousand gallons (178,000 liters) of hydrogen and seventeen thousand gallons (64,000 liters) of oxygen every minute.

The main engines use a staged combustion cycle, meaning that to start the engine, the propellants are burned partially at high pressure and relatively low temperature, then burned completely at high temperature and high pressure in the main combustion chamber. The rapid mixing of the propellants under these conditions is so complete that 99 percent of the fuel provides power.

During the last part of the shuttle's ascent into space, engine thrust is reduced to insure that the acceleration level is no more than three times that of the effect of Earth's gravity. This means that there is less force on the bodies of the astronauts during ascent. While the first astronauts were clad in bulky suits to reduce the impact of this pull, today's astronauts go up wearing simple uniforms.

AMAZING FACTS

Arrangement of sleeping bunks aboard the space shuttle depends on the number of crew on each mission. Some of the crew are always on duty, so that rarely are more than four bunks needed. The first person floats to the top bunk, the second into the lower bunk. The third sleeper's bed is on the reverse side of the lower bunk, facing the floor. The fourth astronaut sleeps on his or her feet, so to speak, with the bunk set up vertically against one end of the two level bunk. With no sensation of up or down, it doesn't make much difference where astronauts sleep, just so long as they tie themselves down.

AMAZING FACTS

The space shuttle lands like a glider without power. There is no chance for another approach when the pilot and onboard computers have committed for the final descent.

Space shuttles now use a drag parachute at the end of a mission. It was introduced in 1992 to reduce the length of the landing run, minimize brake wear, and give improved directional stability in wet and windy conditions.

The shuttle's main engine is the first rocket engine to use a built-in electronic digital controller. The controller will accept commands from the orbiter for engine start, shutdown, and change in throttle setting. In the event of a failure, the controller takes action automatically to control the problem and shut down the engine safely.

All of this technical wizardry has come at a high price. There have been lengthy discussions among rocket experts and scientists as to whether the high cost of shuttle trips is worth the expendable resources of a tightening budget. Some feel that unpiloted rockets could boost satellites into space cheaper than the cost of a space shuttle launch. That is certainly true of some information-gathering satellites, but there will always be a need for hands-on work by astronauts in space. In the not so distant future, plans for more permanent settlements in space will require human construction and maintenance. People with many talents will be needed.

— Chapter 7 —
Our Future in Space

An artist's impression of space station Freedom *shows a space shuttle about to dock. At least eighteen shuttle flights over four years will be required to construct the space station.*

A space station laboratory has been on the minds of many since rockets first broke the barriers of Earth's gravity. President Ronald Reagan finally gave the go-ahead for some of the futuristic models that NASA had been developing. Many computer-generated designs for space station *Freedom*, as it will be called, have been built and tested on Earth, but no one can guess all the difficulties that will be faced when such a tremendous building program is undertaken. Yet scientists and engineers are trying to take as much guesswork out of the planning as they possibly can.

There are many sceptics who doubt that a space station will accomplish all that is claimed for science. Some people believe that the same sort of data can be collected by unpiloted probes at a much lower cost. However, if humans are ever to explore or colonize space, even in the distant future, a space station is needed.

The cost is enormous. Over the past ten years, budgets have been cut dramatically, but a modified plan for the station is still expected to be started, hopefully by the turn of the century.

Carolyn Griner

Carolyn Griner is a flight systems engineer already working on plans for the space station, *Freedom*, which, it is hoped, will eventually be in orbit by the turn of the century. Her responsibilities are broad, involving flight operations and ground operations and training facilities for the space station.

Griner was born in Granite City, Illinois, in 1945, but her family soon moved to Winter Park, Florida. She always was a summer person, she admits, so the southern climate was to her liking. Griner received her science degree in astronautical engineering from Florida State University in 1967. Astronomy was her favorite subject, but she found she could combine down-to-earth engineering classes with stargazing. Her graduate study was in the field of industrial engineering at the University of Alabama in Huntsville,

Carolyn Griner, right, with two colleagues at the Lyndon B. Johnson Space Center, Houston, Texas.

the headquarters of one of NASA's largest research centers.

Before even finishing her advanced degree, she was at work at the Marshall Center, where she served as the main investigator for experiments that would be set up for processing payloads for *Spacelab* — a habitable orbital laboratory, launched by space shuttle. She has also served as the payload operations director for other missions.

Carolyn Griner is a trained scuba diver. She's been able to use her skill for space-related projects as well as for sport and frequently dons a pressurized underwater suit at the Marshall Center's neutral buoyancy simulator. It's a seventy-five-foot wide, fifty-foot deep pool filled with 1.3 million gallons of clear water. A mockup of a space platform with a solar array system has been placed at the bottom of the tank.

Griner's suit has been carefully fitted with just enough weight to keep her from floating to the surface and enough buoyancy to keep her from sinking to the bottom. This is as close to the conditions in outer

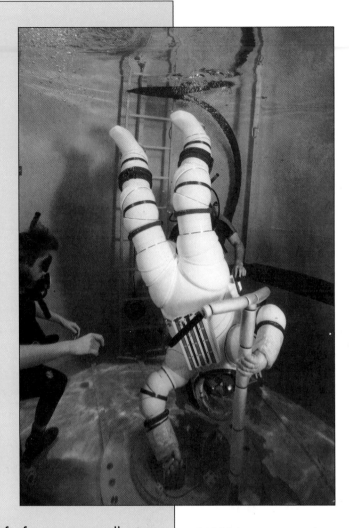

A NASA astronaut trains in the neutral buoyancy simulator at the Marshall Space Flight Center.

space as one can get on Earth. The real outfit for space walks is a close copy of the tank suit. She works underwater to test the right tools for use in zero gravity; clumsy gloves are redesigned to her specifications to make them more manageable. Every motion is programmed to mimic what is needed for specific jobs in space.

Carolyn Griner is one of four women specialists who took part in a simulated five-day space mission at the center. She has also been selected to fly in space aboard the shuttle.

Her technical papers have covered a number of important subjects, from analyzing gases that have been expelled into outer space by the shuttle to the effect of gravity on the growth of branching crystal formations in space. Griner is a member of the National Society of Professional Engineers and the American Institute of Physics.

Plans for *Freedom*

Because the space station will have to be built from parts that can be carried into orbit by the space shuttle, it will be made in sections. In one design, four cylinders, each twenty feet long by fourteen feet wide, make up the station. One cylinder will be living quarters for the astronauts; another will be used as a cargo hold. The other two cylinders will be laboratories, one for scientific research and one for commercially manufactured products that cannot be produced under the weight of Earth's gravity.

There will be a hub on which the shuttle will be able to dock. At least half an acre of solar arrays will provide power. These are lightweight panels that absorb the Sun's rays and convert the heat into electrical power.

A Factory in Space

The space station will consume a lot of that power if it is to be used as a miniature factory to manufacture drugs and alloys. An alloy is a metal made by melting together two or more other metals. In zero gravity, the result is a purer mixture than can be obtained on Earth.

One large drug company plans to use the weightless conditions in space. Researchers have already experimented with the process during space shuttle trials. A liquid is pumped through a long, rectangular box from one end to the other. An electric current is applied from side to side across the box, and this encourages the different components in the liquid to move across the chamber at different rates. By the time the liquid has reached the other end of the chamber, the various components have formed into separate streams of pure material that can be collected separately.

At ground level, gravity interferes with the separation. Experiments on the shuttle have proved that in space, up to seven hundred times more of the substances to be collected can be produced than on Earth, and in a much purer state. The company

---

AMAZING FACTS

Since 1960, NASA has been responsible for launching more than 180 scientific, weather, and communications spacecraft, along with some military satellites.

AMAZING FACTS

The ultimate in propulsion would power a ship that travels at the speed of light. The speed is theoretically achieved from energy released by the destruction of matter by antimatter.

believes that up to ten new products could be manufactured in this way, including a new treatment for diabetes and new proteins and enzymes to treat a range of medical disorders.

A Launching Base

But the space station is definitely not just a commercial venture. Engineers want a base from which they can move into other areas of space to retrieve satellites for repair and refueling. NASA has been planning a new type of spacecraft that would need only a fraction of the power a space shuttle uses to operate. These space tugs, as they are being called, would be able to deliver satellites into orbit that would be out of reach for the shuttle.

Space station Freedom, *with a cutaway view of the U.S. laboratory module. To its left is the European Space Agency's module, with Japan's module behind it. Immediately behind the U.S. module is the common habitation module that will provide sleeping, washing, and eating facilities.*

Lonnie Reid

Dr. Lonnie Reid was born in Gastonia, North Carolina, where he spent his early childhood. His was a farming family, and he's always had great respect for those who work the land. It was not a rich life, but the family certainly wasn't one of the poorer ones in the community.

What set Reid apart was his curiosity, his love of school, his thirst for books. He was forever reading. He chose not just one subject, but just about anything he could get his hands on. He liked scientific subjects the best, but no one ever called Reid a drudge. He was popular with his classmates and starred on the high school football team. Still, college seemed a long way off.

Lonnie started a search for his own destiny by serving a tour of duty with the U.S. Army in Korea. He was there for sixteen months, finding that horizons of learning could be stretched over geographical boundaries.

After his tour of duty, he entered Tennessee State University in Nashville on a football scholarship. He still held down part-time jobs for spending money but was able to earn topnotch grades in all his subjects. He received a bachelor of science degree in mechanical engineering and was immediately recruited by officials of NASA to join their science research program.

In 1961, Reid started working at the NASA Lewis Research Center in Cleveland, Ohio. Through their graduate study program, he earned a master of science degree in mechanical engineering and later a Ph.D. in engineering science from the University of Toledo in Ohio.

Dr. Reid's present title is chief of the internal fluid mechanics division of Lewis Research Center. That translates to being in charge of improving and redesigning aerospace propulsion systems that may one day take us into deep space. He has already seen the results of his work in the remarkable accomplishments NASA has been able to achieve in its current flights into space.

His division is staffed with about 120 employees, mostly scientists and engineers with advanced degrees. Reid sets himself a tough schedule to follow, but having a likeable and understanding boss has prompted his staff to follow the same rigorous regime.

In 1989, Dr. Reid was awarded the NASA Exceptional Service award for his work on the technology of rocket engines. But perhaps his most important work takes place after office hours. As an African-American, Dr. Reid serves as an inspiration to many young, would-be scientists of the future. He has served for many years as a math tutor for inner-city students. His greatest talent is making young people enjoy the subject, giving them a hint of exciting careers that require mathematical skills.

The Lewis Research Center, Cleveland, Ohio, where Lonnie Reid is chief of the internal fluid mechanics division.

Technicians assemble a test prototype of a new Ariane rocket engine in France. Ariane is the European space rocket built by about sixty companies in ten western European countries. It was designed to place satellites in geostationary orbit.

Such a vehicle is being developed and will be able to travel between low Earth orbit, a couple of hundred miles above the Earth, and the geostationary orbit, some 22,300 miles high, where most communication satellites are located. These geostationary satellites travel at the speed needed to keep pace with the rotation of the Earth — so they seem to remain "stationary" over a specific area of our world. In spite of their movement and that of the Earth, they always seem to be directly overhead.

However, the service and repair functions that engineers desire from a space station don't jibe easily with what scientists want. Many scientific experiments need a platform that won't be affected by contamination from nearby rocket engines. But this need can be met by building platforms orbiting at a distance from the main space station.

Exploring Other Worlds

The space station must also act as a base where future missions to the Moon and to the planets can be marshalled and from where they can be launched. People will have to live many years aboard the space station to gather enough research data to attempt deep-space exploration.

Space station *Freedom* is a crucial step for future missions to colonize the Moon and to explore Mars. The station will teach us how to build, operate, and maintain the complex systems that are necessary to sustain life on a permanent basis in the hostile environment of space.

What Will Come Next?

How are we going to reach distant planets? Some ideas remain wishful fantasy for the moment, but who is to say that we might not be transported on beams of light? Even now it is possible for beams of laser light, sent from Earth, to strike mirrors aboard spacecraft that would redirect the beam onto the propellant for ignition.

If we can make atomic energy safer, with no worries about the harmful effects of radiation or the disposal of used radioactive fuel rods, we may have an abundance of fuel that delivers a much higher thrust. Nuclear power could send rockets farther and faster than before. Or if we could harness the energy of the Sun, spacecraft may one day hoist their solar sails to catch the gentle force of solar radiation.

Electric propulsion has always been a possibility once a more powerful propellant has sent a rocket into orbit. With little weight, and fuel consumption at a minimum, interplanetary travel may depend on this form of energy.

In the meantime, it has been the rocket, that wonderful instrument discovered by some Chinese inventor of long ago, that has made our space age possible.

The end of the first flight of the Delta Clipper prototype in 1993. The aim is to create a reusable, single-stage rocket that will provide a cheap and reliable way to launch satellites into orbit. This prototype rose 160 feet, moved 320 feet to one side while hovering, then landed vertically on its four retractable legs.

Timeline

100 B.C. — Gunpowder in use in China.

A.D. 1231 — Rockets are used in warfare.

March, 1926 — Robert Goddard successfully tests the first rocket using liquid fuel.

1937–1944 — German scientists develop the V-2 rocket.

October, 1957 — USSR puts *Sputnik I*, the first artificial satellite, into space.

January, 1958 — United States launches *Explorer I*, its first artificial satellite.

March, 1958 — American satellite *Vanguard I* is the first to use solar power.

October, 1959 — USSR photographs far side of the Moon for the first time.

April, 1961 — USSR puts first man, Yuri Gagarin, in space.

May, 1961 — Alan Shepard becomes first American in space.

February, 1962 — John Glenn is the first American to orbit the Earth.

December, 1962 — U.S. probe *Mariner 2* flies past Venus on the first successful interplanetary mission.

July, 1963 — USSR sends first woman, Valentina Tereshkova, into space.

March, 1965 — USSR's Alexei Leonov performs the first space walk.

June, 1965 — Edward White becomes the first American to walk in space.

December, 1965 — *Gemini 6* and *7* rendezvous in orbit.

February, 1966 — USSR's *Luna 9* makes first controlled landing on the Moon.

July, 1969 — American first piloted lunar landing, *Apollo 11*.

May, 1973 — Launching of American unpiloted space lab, *Skylab*, damaged during takeoff.

July, 1975 — Soviet and American spacecraft dock while in orbit.

December, 1979 — First flight of Ariane, Europe's satellite launcher.

April, 1981 — First flight of the space shuttle *Columbia*.

February, 1986 — Soviet space station *Mir* launched.

April, 1990 — Hubble Space Telescope launched.

Further Reading

Baird, Anne. *The U.S. Space Camp Book of Rockets.* New York: Murrow Junior Books, 1991.

Berger, Melvin. *Space Shots, Shuttles, and Satellites.* New York: G. P. Putnam's Sons, 1983.

Branley, Franklyn M. *From Sputnik to Space Shuttles.* New York: Thomas Y. Crowell, 1986.

Dolan, Edward F. *Famous Firsts in Space.* New York: E. P. Dutton, 1989.

Kennedy, Gregory P. *The First Men in Space.* New York and Philadelphia: Chelsea House Publications, 1991.

Lampton, Christopher. *Wernher von Braun.* New York: Franklin Watts, 1985.

Vogt, Gregory. *The Twenty-Fifth Anniversary Album of NASA.* New York: Franklin Watts, 1983.

Vogt, Gregory. *Apollo and the Moon Landing.* Brookfield, CT: Millbrook Press, 1991.

Glossary

Ballistic Missile: A missile launched by a rocket engine that becomes a free-falling object as it reaches its target.

Cryogenic: Comes from a Greek word meaning "ice cold." Refers to liquid oxygen and liquid hydrogen, which must be kept at supercool temperatures so they do not revert to gas.

Fuselage: The central body of the aircraft, where the crew and cargo are. The wings and tail are attached to the fuselage.

Hypergolic: Referring to a type of fuel that ignites on contact with oxygen.

Intercontinental Ballistic Missile (ICBM): A missile designed for long distances.

Lunar Roving Vehicle: Space vehicle used on the Moon.

Magnetic field: A space surrounding a magnet or an electric conductor carrying a current, in which a magnetic force can be detected.

Mass: The quantity of material an object contains. It is also a measure of the object's resistance to motion. Unlike weight, mass is constant, not affected by the force of gravity.

Neutral buoyancy simulator: A water tank in which astronauts train to get them used to zero gravity.

Orbiter: The part of the space shuttle that flies like a plane.

Orbiting: Traveling around the Earth.

Propellant: For rockets this means both fuel and oxidizer.

Retrorockets: Rockets aimed in opposite direction to the forward thrust of a rocket to help brake the movement of a spacecraft.

Satellite: An object in space revolving around a larger object.

Sounding rockets: Rockets sent aloft to analyze atmospheric conditions. They are not in orbit.

Thrust: The force that propels a rocket.

Turbojet: A jet engine run by a stream of gas or liquid that moves against its blades and moves them.

Index

Numbers in *italic* indicate pictures; numbers in **bold** indicate biographies